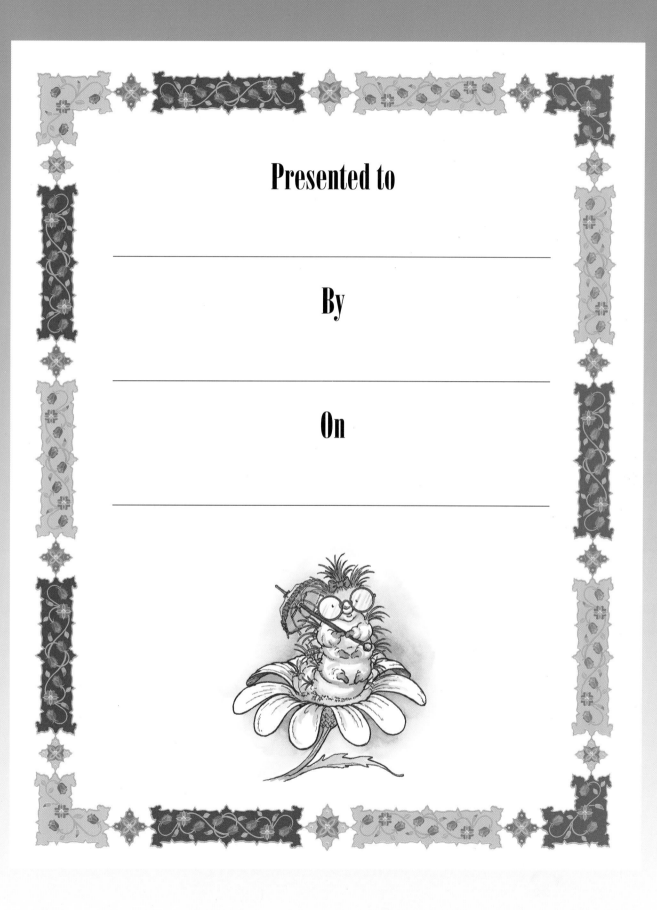

Presented to

_____

By

_____

On

_____

I'd Choose You!

by John Trent, Ph.D.
illustrated by Judy Love

WORD PUBLISHING
Dallas·London·Vancouver·Melbourne

I'd Choose You!

Text © 1994 by John Trent, Ph.D
Illustrations © 1994 by Judy Love

The Scripture quotation at the end of this book is from the
New International Version of the Bible (NIV), copyright © 1978 by
the New York International Bible Society.

Managing Editor: Laura Minchew
Project Editor: Beverly Philllips

Library of Congress Cataloging-in-Publicaton Data

Trent, John T.
  I'd choose you! / by John Trent; illustrated by Judy Love.
    p. cm.
  Summary: When Little Elephant tells his mother about his bad day,
she helps him realize just how special he is to her and to God.
  ISBN 0–8499–1165–6
[1. Self-esteem—Fiction. 2. Parent and child—Fiction.
Judy, 1953–   ill. II. Title.
PZ7.T71945Id   1994
[E]—dc20   94–28371
                                                           CIP
                                                            AC

PRINTED IN THE UNITED STATES OF AMERICA

97 98 99 LBM 9 8 7 6

To Kari and Laura,
our two precious daughters
that God has loaned us to love and bless—
We couldn't be more thankful for you
or more proud of who you're becoming in Him.
You've heard it a thousand times
since you were born, but we mean it…
"Out of all the kids in the world, we'd choose you."

—JOHN TRENT

❧ ❧ ❧ ❧

To Kathy, who gives so much and expects so little in
return, and to her daughter Chris, who will help bring
the blessing to children through teaching.

—JUDY LOVE

A Note to Parents on Blessing Your Children

YEARS AGO, when our oldest daughter, Kari, was three years old, it took three tries one night to get her to bed. First came stories and prayers. Then, a glass of water. Then her blanket had fallen on the floor. Just when we thought she was down for the night, her voice rang down the hallway.

"Night, Mom. Night, Dad. *And don't forget to bless me in the morning!*"

At three years old, Kari was looking forward to something that children have longed for since Old Testament times—their parents' "blessing."

For us, it's been a morning event for Kari and her sister, Laura, each day of their lives. It's not a ritual, but it's not something complicated or confusing, either. It's just five simple steps outlined in the Bible that can leave a lasting, positive memory in a child's life.

I teach seminars across the country and have co-authored a book for adults—*The Gift of the Blessing*—on this powerful, life-changing concept. But for years, parents have asked me to put this message in "kids' language."

That's what I've done in this book. *I'd Choose You* is a fun story that also contains all five elements of the Old Testament blessing. It's an easy way for you to share the concept of the "Blessing" with your little ones, and for them to begin to understand its power to "bless" their lives.

In this story, you'll see the elements of *appropriate, meaningful touch*, like a big, loving hug; *spoken words of affirmation*, represented by "cheers"; and *attaching high value* to someone, as seen in the "You're Someone Special Medal." You'll also see the need to *picture a special future* for kids (who often hear parents' predictions about their future with literal effect), and to make a *genuine commitment* to include the blessing as a regular part of their lives.

Each morning, our children, Kari and Laura, have received something as simple as combining these five elements into a few moments of focused attention. We sit next to them, or simply lay our hands on them, and say something like,

"Lord may you bless Kari and Laura, today. May you help them to know how much you love them, and what a wonderful future you have for them. Thank you for all the warmth and love you've put in their lives, and how kind and strong they're both becoming.

*"And Lord, may they always know that we love them . . . and—that out of all the kids in the world—**we'd choose them.** Amen."*

The blessing isn't a formula. But it does have specific ingredients. It's spoken in love . . . shared with a loving touch . . . and stirred by God's wondrous love, which we desire to communicate. That's a recipe for building a positive future in any child's life! And it's one I hope you'll use and enjoy as you read this story about Norbert the Little Elephant. This little fellow and his parents can teach us giant-sized truths that will build loving, lasting memories.

John Trent, Ph.D.,
President,
Encouraging Words

Norbert the Little Elephant had a very sad look on his face as he slowly walked up the steps to his house.

This had
been the
worst day
of his
whole life.

"Mom, it's been an awful day. Nothing's gone right since I left for school this morning," said Norbert.

"You didn't miss the roller coaster again did you?" his mother asked. (For where they lived, all the kids took roller coasters to school instead of buses.)

"No, I got to the roller coaster stop just in time, but everyone else already had someone to sit with. And I had to sit all by myself on the very last row."

"And then at lunch, all the fifth-graders decided they wanted to sit at the table by the window. And that meant the only place left to sit was with Heidi the Hippo!"

"But Heidi's a nice girl," Norbert's mother said.

"Mom, she thinks she's my girlfriend. She even tried to put her head on my shoulder. It was so awful! She lost her balance and fell in my mashed potatoes! *Right in front of the fifth-graders!*"

"Then after school, I went out to play ball, and when they picked teams, there was one kid too many."

"You," said his mother, quietly.

"Yes, me. Nobody likes me. Nobody wants to pick me."
And as he spoke, a big tear rolled

down

his

trunk.

"Norbert," his mother said, in her softest, warmest voice. "If I could use my arms to hug only one child, guess which one I'd choose?"

"That's easy," said Little Elephant. "You'd choose Puffy Panda. He's so-o-o-o soft, everyone likes to hug him. And since Puffy is so-o-o-o big, everybody can hug him! . . . all at the same time."

"No-o-o-o," Mother smiled. "Guess again. If I could give a *'You're Someone Special!'* medal to only one child . . . guess which one I'd choose?"

"Mom, you'd choose Florence the Flamingo. She deserves a medal because she's the only one who can do a triple loop when we all go ice-skating."

"No-o-o-o," said Norbert's mom. "Guess again.
If I could use my voice to cheer for only one child,
guess which one I'd choose?"

"That's easy, too. You'd choose Ralph the Rhino.
Everybody cheers for him because he's so brave. He even
jumps off the high diving board."

"No-o-o-o," said Mother. "Guess again. If I could help just one child realize what an exciting and wonderful future God has for him . . . a future where he can become anything he wants to be . . . guess which one I'd choose?"

"Mom, that's a no-brainer. You'd choose Cassie the Caterpillar because she'll be a beautiful butterfly someday."

"No-o-o-o, not Cassie the Caterpillar," Mother chuckled. . . .

"If I could use my arms each day to hug and my voice to cheer . . .

"If I could honor one child who has an exciting and wonderful future . . .

"And if I could teach him each day that he is God's special gift, especially on those days when he doesn't get picked . . .

"Guess which one I'd choose every time? . . .

"I'd choose YOU!"

"And I'd choose you, too!" said Father Elephant, who had just come in the door.

"Daddy!" Norbert the Elephant yelled as he ran to hug his father.

"And we're not the only ones who would choose you," said his father with a smile.

"Really?" asked Norbert.

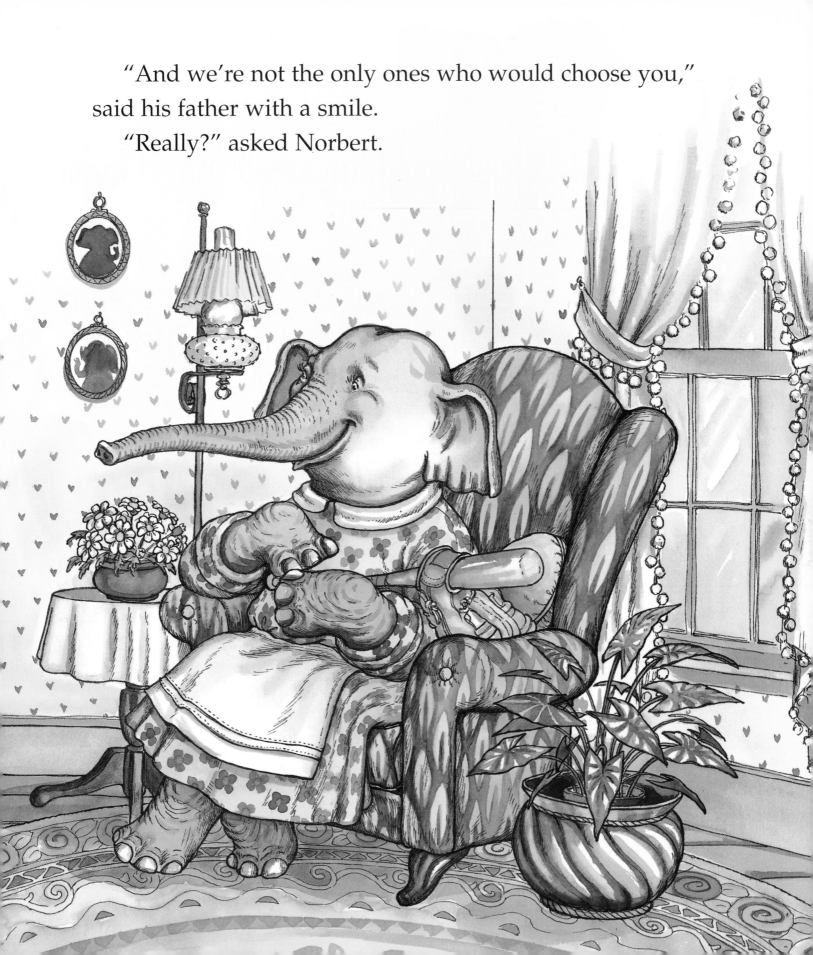

"Heidi the Hippo is outside with ice cream, and she's waiting for **YOU!**" said Father.

"Oh, no-o-o-o!" Norbert gasped.

> "For you are a people holy to the Lord your God. The Lord your God has chosen you out of all the people on the face of the earth to be his people, his treasured possession."

DEUTERONOMY 7:6

You'll Choose These...

...Popular Releases from John Trent